What's the Story?

50 Photographs and 1,000 Ideas to Inspire Creative Writing

John Sheirer

ISBN: 978-0-9904872-1-0

All photos by John Sheirer
Cover by Christopher Reilley

Also by John Sheirer:

Libby Speaks: The Wit and Wisdom of the World's Wisest Dog
Tales of a Real American Liberal
One Bite: Stories for Short Attention Spans, Stolen Moments, and Busy Lives
Loop Year: 365 Days on the Trail
Growing Up Mostly Normal in the Middle of Nowhere: A Memoir
Saying My Name: Selected Poems, 1982-2002
Shut Up and Speak!

Published in the United States by Big Table Publishing Company.

Big Table Publishing Company
Boston, MA
www.bigtablepublishing.com

For all of my supportive colleagues at Asnuntuck Community College

Introduction

All authors struggle with inspiration from time to time. Whether a beginner or a seasoned professional, we've all had our share of writer's block. We've all stared at the computer screen and ordered another espresso in a noisy coffee shop, chewed on our #2 yellow pencils while fidgeting in a uncomfortable school desk, or sat on the back porch with our leather-bound journal listening to the birds. We've all known we could write–if only we could get started.

This book is filled with photographs of intriguing scenes, people, objects, and situations to help inspire you to write. Each photo has ten "background questions" to stimulate your imagination and memory, five "What's the Story?" writing prompts to help you shape and develop your ideas, and five "first lines" to jump-start your creativity. That's 1,000 ideas to help break any writer's block.

When photographers take pictures, they don't just randomly point their camera. They try to frame the photo to engage a viewer and stimulate thoughts and feelings. The photo might show a captivating place, a fascinating person, an unusual view of an object, or an active event. Frame and focus are also writerly concerns. Writers use words to capture places, people, things, and events that will grab a reader's attention, focus thoughts and emotions, and frame a perspective.

Writers get most of our inspiration from the people, objects, and events in the world around us. We've developed the skill of looking very closely at our surroundings and asking questions about what we observe. These questions often help us use our imagination and memory to come up with ideas for writing. Whether the genre is fiction, poetry, or personal essay, the photos and ideas in this book will give you a place to begin.

You can start this book at the beginning and move along page-by-page, open it at random and jump around, or simply write about the photographs that most capture your interest. And each piece you write will build your skill for finding and developing writing ideas in everything that happens around you as you continue to ask, "What's the Story?"

So... What's the Story?

Background Questions

1) How old is the baseball player?
2) Give the player and coach names or nicknames that hint at something in their personality.
3) How did he get to third base?
4) Is he an average player, a benchwarmer, or a star?
5) Are his parents watching?
6) What inning is it?
7) Is his team ahead, behind, or tied?
8) Is the coach whispering or yelling?
9) What is the team's record of wins and losses?
10) What is the coach's day job?

What's the Story?

1) Write a dialogue of the conversation between the player and the coach as they talk about something completely unrelated to the baseball game.
2) Write a narrative about how the player got to third base and what happens when the next player bats. Make the action very vivid and detailed.
3) Write a dialogue between the player's parents as they watch the game.
4) Write an internal monologue of the player's thoughts about this game just before he falls asleep that night.
5) Write about an exciting or disappointing moment that you have experienced while playing a sport.

Bonus: Make up your own story, poem, or essay inspired by this photo.

First Lines

1) Roger had never hit a triple before.
2) *I wish Coach Johnson would stop yelling at me!* Bob thought.
3) Mom and Dad said they would be there, but I was almost too scared to turn around and look for them.
4) "Hey, number 23!" someone shouted from the stands.
5) "Ice cream or pizza after the game?"

Background Questions

1) What kind of person is the bike's owner?
2) What is the owner doing while the bike is locked up on the street?
3) Is the bike new or old?
4) Why is the owner riding a bike in the snow?
5) What is in the storage compartment on the back of the bike?
6) How long has the bike been parked on the street?
7) Is this a big city or a small town?
8) Is this an area with stores and businesses or homes?
9) What will happen to the bike if no one comes to get it?
10) What's in the drink bottle?

What's the Story?

1) Write an internal monologue the thoughts of someone looking at this bike and thinking about stealing it.
2) Narrate and describe what it would be like to ride a bike on a cold day with snow on the ground, paying particular attention to the sensory details..
3) Imagine this bike could talk. How would it describe the way its owner treats it?
4) Write about a person whose car wouldn't start in the morning and had to ride his or her kid's bike to work.
5) Write about a time you did something really unusual, such as riding a bike in the winter or sledding on a muddy hill in the summer.

Bonus: Make up your own story, poem, or essay inspired by this photo.

First Lines

1) Susan had no idea why her mom's bike was parked outside the school that afternoon.
2) The icy sidewalk would be dangerous, but I had to ride home as fast as possible.
3) The bike looked vaguely familiar.
4) Three days of rain had melted most of the snow.
5) The blood from Mark's knee soaked into the snow.

Background Questions

1) Is this coffeepot-shaped building a house or a business?
2) If it's a house, who lives in it?
3) If it's a business, what kind of business?
4) What would be a good name for the business in this building?
5) How long has it been since anyone has been inside this building?
6) What do the people who live in the other buildings think of the coffeepot?
7) Is this in a rural area, a small town, or a big city?
8) What's in the U-Haul?
9) Are people moving into the building or moving out of it?
10) What other odd-shaped buildings might be in this neighborhood?

What's the Story?

1) Write a dialogue between this building's designer and his or her children on the day the designer got the idea for shaping a building like a coffeepot.
2) Imagine this building can talk. What would it say on the day before it was scheduled to be torn down?
3) Describe what the inside of this building looks like now or when the building was new.
4) Write about your own family moving into this building to live or to open a business.
5) Describe the strangest building near where you live. What makes it unusual?

<u>Bonus</u>: Make up your own story, poem, or essay inspired by this photo.

First Lines

1) I wasn't sure what she meant when she said we should meet at a place called "The Coffee Pot."
2) Melanie had grown up in a strange house.
3) The moving van arrived at daybreak.
4) The neighborhood had changed a lot in the last few years.
5) "It's a surprise," he said with a sly smile on his face.

Background Questions

1) Give this woman a name.
2) What kind of a place is this?
3) What time of day is this?
4) Is she at work?
5) What is her job?
6) Does she usually work alone or with others?
7) Where are her coworkers?
8) Is she good at her job?
9) How long has she had this job?
10) Why is she smiling?

What's the Story?

1) This woman appears to be very happy. Write about what happened at her job that made her this happy.
2) Imagine someone very angry comes up to this happy woman for help. Write a dialogue of their conversation.
3) Write a monologue of this woman's thoughts during her most boring day on the job.
4) Imagine that she is doing something on her computer that has nothing to do with her job. Write about what she is doing and how she tries to hide it from her coworkers.
5) Write about a time you interacted with someone who was helping you as part of his or her job.

Bonus: Make up your own story, poem, or essay inspired by this photo.

First Lines

1) She wasn't going to like what he had to say.
2) How many times had this happened?
3) He didn't know what would have happened if she hadn't smiled at him that day.
4) He tried to remember the name of the song playing on the speakers in the background.
5) "That's unusual."

Background Questions

1) What is this boy's name?
2) Where are his parents?
3) What kind of event is happening behind him?
4) Is he happy and excited to be here or is he bored and sad?
5) Does he have many friends or just a few close friends?
6) The setting looks like a dock beside a large body of water. Does he come here often or is this his first visit?
7) Is he looking at boats in the water?
8) Does he have brothers and sisters?
9) Does he like school?
10) Did one of his parents pick out the shirt he is wearing or did he?

What's the Story?

1) Assume the boy is looking off the dock into a large body of water like an ocean, river, or lake. Write an internal monologue of his thoughts as he gazes into the water.
2) Write a dialogue between the boy's grandparents as they watch him on the dock.
3) Imagine that the event happening behind him is his own birthday party. Write about why he walked away from his own party?
4) Describe all of the sounds the boy hears around him.
5) Describe how you felt the first time you saw a particular ocean, river, or lake. If you've never seen one, write about what you imagine it would be like.

Bonus: Make up your own story, poem, or essay inspired by this photo.

First Lines

1) *I'm big enough to do it myself,* Randy thought as he gazed at the rowboat.
2) He couldn't understand why the older kids picked on him so much.
3) The music was louder than he had expected.
4) "Hi, what's your name?"
5) Wally didn't know that bad weather was coming soon.

Background Questions

1) How long has this house been empty?
2) How many rooms does this house have?
3) How many people lived in the house before it became empty?
4) What were the names of the people who lived in the house?
5) How old is this house?
6) Is this house in a rural area, small town, or city?
7) Do many cars drive by this house?
8) What was the weather like on the day this photograph was taken?
9) What are the neighboring buildings like?
10) Is this house haunted?

What's the Story?

1) Narrate and describe what it was like years ago when the parents told the kids who lived here that they were going to move away.
2) Imagine a family of two parents and two children stopped their car in front of this house to look at it. Write a dialogue of the conversation the family would have as they sat in the car and looked at the house.
3) Imagine you and three friends are trapped by a storm or other natural disaster and are forced to stay overnight in this house. Narrate and describe an important moment from that night.
4) Imagine the people who lived here left some of their possessions in this house. Describe what they left and why they left it.
5) Describe how you felt when you moved from a place you really liked. Or, if you've lived in the same place all your life, describe how you imagine you would feel if you had to move.

Bonus: Make up your own story, poem, or essay inspired by this photo.

First Lines

1) They couldn't believe what they found in the basement of the old house.
2) Linda hadn't been to her childhood home in twenty years.
3) It was almost dark when they found the candles.
4) The wind sounded like voices calling out to them.
5) "This is going to be a big job!"

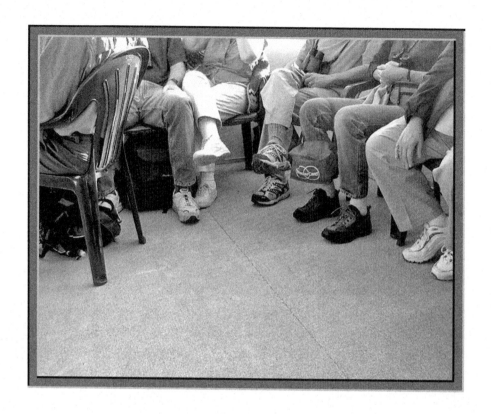

Background Questions

1) How many people can you see?
2) How many are men and how many are women?
3) How old are they?
4) What time of day is it?
5) What month of the year is it?
6) What kind of place is this?
7) What do their shoes have in common?
8) How well do these people know each other?
9) Do these people seem happy or sad, friendly or angry?
10) Are these people talking with each other or silent?

What's the Story?

1) Notice that some of the people have binoculars. Describe what they might be looking at though those binoculars.
2) Assume these people have never met before and are not sitting together by choice. Write a dialogue of the conversation they might be having.
3) Describe the faces of each of these people.
4) Assume one of these people has just realized that he or she is in the wrong place but can't leave. Write an internal monologue of that person's thoughts.
5) Narrate and describe a time when you were crowded in a small space with other people. What did you do? How did the situation make you feel?

Bonus: Make up your own story, poem, or essay inspired by this photo.

First Lines

1) "It's nice to meet you," she said.
2) Howard had never been anyplace like this before.
3) *I really wish I had gone to the bathroom first,* he thought.
4) The view was amazing.
5) *Why is she staring at me?* Carol thought.

Background Questions

1) What is this woman's name?
2) How old is she?
3) What is she writing or drawing in the window?
4) What kind of business is this?
5) Does she enjoy her job?
6) How long has she worked here?
7) What is the weather like?
8) How many people walk by her window in a typical minute?
9) What does it say on the board outside the window?
10) What are the people inside doing while she works on the window?

What's the Story?

1) Write an internal monologue of this woman's thoughts as she works on the store window.
2) Assume that it's hard to hear through the glass. Write a dialogue of the conversation between this woman and someone looking in the window trying to talk with her.
3) Write a letter from this woman to a friend telling about something surprising that happened while she was working in the window.
4) Make a list of all the jobs this woman had before she got this job and describe the duties of those jobs.
5) Narrate and describe an interesting encounter you had with someone working in a store or on the sidewalk outside a store.

Bonus: Make up your own story, poem, or essay inspired by this photo.

First Lines

1) "Hey, Andrea, how much longer is this going to take?"
2) The woman in the window looked so much like Sally–but she wasn't Sally.
3) Life is unpredictable.
4) The glass was smooth and surprisingly cool to the touch.
5) *Why do I always get stuck with the hard jobs?* Yolanda thought.

Background Questions

1) What is this boy's name?
2) What kind of room is he in?
3) What is he doing?
4) What was he doing right before he went into this room?
5) What is he going to do when he leaves this room?
6) Does he seem angry or amused about being surprised?
7) Is this in his home or is he visiting somewhere else?
8) Does he have brothers and sisters?
9) What time of day this happening?
10) Do you think he used soap when he washed his hands?

What's the Story?

1) Describe the strangest bathroom you can imagine.

2) Write an internal monologue of the thoughts of someone who really has to use the bathroom but is stuck waiting outside the door while his brother or sister is inside taking too much time.

3) Write the dialogue of a conversation between two friends who get in trouble and are assigned cleaning the bathroom as their punishment.

4) Write a list of everything you can think of that might be in a typical bathroom, and then add a few things that are not usually found in a bathroom. Explain why these unusual items are in the bathroom.

5) Have you ever been surprised by someone? Describe the situation and explore exactly why you were surprised, how it felt, how you responded, and what the other person thought of your surprise.

Bonus: Make up your own story, poem, or essay inspired by this photo.

First Lines

1) "Boo!"

2) Shawn really wanted to get back to the party.

3) "I'll be out in a minute!" Jerry shouted again.

4) Sometimes the strangest things happen when you're not expecting them.

5) The sudden knock at the door made Kevin spin around in surprise.

Background Questions

1) What are these two boys' names?
2) How old are they?
3) Whose yard are they in?
4) What's at the top of the tree?
5) How did it get there?
6) Are these boys friends or do they dislike each other?
7) Are they talking to each other?
8) Is anyone else watching them?
9) Will the boy be able to climb to the top of the tree?
10) Do the branches look strong enough to hold the boy without breaking?

What's the Story?

1) Narrate the story of how the hat ended up in the top of the tree.
2) Write an internal monologue of what the boy on the ground is thinking as he watches the other boy climb the tree.
3) Write a dialogue between two neighbors as they watch these boys from a window in the house across the street.
4) Write a dialogue between the two boys as they decide which one will climb the tree to get the hat.
5) Have you ever climbed a tree? Write about what it was like. If you haven't, write about what you image it would be like.

Bonus: Make up your own story, poem, or essay inspired by this photo.

First Lines

1) The wind picked up speed as Josh approached the top of the tree.
2) The hat had been a gift from his father.
3) "Are you sure your mom said this was okay?"
4) "How did that get up there?'
5) Glen had to hurry because the school bus would be there any minute.

Background Questions

1) What is this rabbit's name?
2) Who are the rabbit's owners?
3) How long has the rabbit been a pet in this house?
4) What do rabbits like to eat?
5) Do you think this rabbit would like to share his cage with another rabbit?
6) Do rabbits make good pets?
7) Are there any other pets in the house?
8) When was the last time the rabbit was fed and given fresh water?
9) Does this rabbit like to watch television?
10) Would you like to crawl into the cage with the rabbit?

What's the Story?

1) Imagine this rabbit could talk. What would he say to you as he looked out of his cage at you?

2) Write about a young child who has been told by his or her parents not to take this rabbit out of the cage—but who takes it out anyway.

3) Narrate and describe what it would be like if this rabbit escaped from his cage and got out of the house.

4) Write a dialogue between a child who really wants a pet rabbit and his or her parents who really don't want to get one.

5) Write about your pets at home. What would they say to you if they could talk? What adventures would they experience if they got out? If you have no pets, write about what kinds you would like and what you would do with them.

Bonus: Make up your own story, poem, or essay inspired by this photo.

First Lines

1) The humans had been gone longer than usual.

2) *Today will be different,* Mr. Whiskers thought as he awoke from a good night's sleep.

3) "Do you think he ever gets tired of rabbit food?" Leah asked her mother.

4) "Hello? Mr. Cat? Are you there?"

5) The door slowly opened.

Background Questions

1) Why is this bus empty?
2) How long does it take this bus to drive its route to school?
3) What is the bus driver's name?
4) Is this an old bus or a new one?
5) How many kids generally ride this bus each day?
6) Does this bus serve kids who live in a city, a small town, or in a rural area?
7) Does this bus take kids anywhere besides school (sporting events, for example)?
8) Do the kids keep the bus clean or is there under the seats?
9) Are the kids usually quiet or loud?
10) What is the best seat to sit in on this bus?

What's the Story?

1) Imagine this bus could talk. What would it say about its driver and the kids who ride in it?

2) Write a dialogue between two kids scrunched down in the back seat having a secret conversation that they don't want anyone else on the crowed bus to hear.

3) Write an internal monologue of the thoughts of the last kid on the bus at the end of its route. Imagine something really important happened in school that day, and the kid has to tell his or her parents about it.

4) Write about a group of kids clustered together in a couple of seats as they tell ghost stories to try to scare each other.

5) Write about a particularly interesting event that happened to you while riding in a bus.

Bonus: Make up your own story, poem, or essay inspired by this photo.

First Lines

1) The door was open just a crack.

2) "What's that smell?"

3) The crying was so soft that Karen barely heard it.

4) His favorite books as a kid were The Magic School Bus stories.

5) *Just one more day*, Bob thought.

Background Questions

1) What are these two kayakers names?
2) How old are they?
3) Do they know each other, and, if so, how?
4) Where are they kayaking?
5) Have they kayaked a lot before or are they trying it for the first time?
6) Are they just starting out or finishing their excursion?
7) Do these people like each other?
8) How deep is the water?
9) Can they see the shoreline from where they are?
10) Are any fish or other marine life swimming around them?

What's the Story?

1) Imagine these people have never been kayaking before and are afraid of tipping over or falling out. Write an internal monologue of their frightened thoughts and describe their actions as they pretend not to be scared.
2) Write a dialogue between the two kayakers as they tell a story about the abandoned bridge in front of them.
3) Write about their experience as if they are strangers who have just met and are lost and worried about finding their way home before dark.
4) Narrate and describe them having lunch together as they sit side-by-side in their kayaks.
5) Write about a particularly interesting experience you have had while out on the water.

Bonus: Make up your own story, poem, or essay inspired by this photo.

First Lines

1) "We need to talk," she said.
2) They didn't know what was swimming only two feet below the water.
3) No one had ever gone farther than the old bridge.
4) *It's so hot,* he thought.
5) They might never see each other again.

Background Questions

1) How far down is it off the edge of this cliff?
2) Where is this cliff located?
3) Give a name to the town below.
4) What time of day is this?
5) What season of the year is this?
6) How wide is the rocky trail that goes along the edge of the cliff?
7) Is this a well-traveled trail, or do very few people walk along this cliff?
8) What is the scene like to the right, out of the picture frame?
9) How far do people have to hike to get to this cliff?
10) What sounds can you hear while standing of the edge of the cliff?

What's the Story?

1) Write a dialogue between two hikers, one who wants to walk along the edge of this cliff and one who doesn't.
2) Write about a group of four people who bring their lunch here and sit on the edge of the cliff to eat it. The one subject they don't mention during lunch (even though they probably all think about it) is they fact that they are on the edge of a cliff.
3) Write about someone looking up from the valley below with binoculars trying to find someone hiking along the edge of this cliff.
4) Write about someone making a cell phone call from the edge of this cliff.
5) Write about a particularly interesting experience you had while hiking, or about an experience where you were in a place that could have been dangerous if you weren't careful.

<u>Bonus</u>: Make up your own story, poem, or essay inspired by this photo.

First Lines

1) "The trail goes where?"
2) *I can see my house from here,* Edgar thought.
3) Roberta usually didn't pay attention when people dared her to do something.
4) Nate was certain that the map led him to this spot.
5) This was a bad moment for the wind to get stronger.

Background Questions

1) How many steps can you see?
2) What kind of building is this?
3) How old is this building?
4) Does a similar staircase go up from this level?
5) How far under the ground does this staircase go?
6) Where does the lighting in this photo come from?
7) Is it day or night outside the building?
8) Whose foot is poking into the bottom of the photo?
9) Is the person about to go down the staircase or has he or she just come up?
10) What is the person feeling as he or she looks down the staircase?

What's the Story?

1) Imagine this stairway leads to a magical fantasy world. Describe that world.
2) Describe what it would be like to run down this staircase with someone chasing you.
3) Write a dialogue between the person at the top of this staircase and an unseen person several levels below.
4) Suppose your pet wandered away and is lost in this building, and you think it might have gone down these stairs into a dark and strange place. Write about what you would do as you searched for your pet.
5) Have you ever walked up of down a cramped staircase like this? Was it scary, uncomfortable, fun, or exciting? Write about what that experience was like for you.

Bonus: Make up your own story, poem, or essay inspired by this photo.

First Lines

1) Shryesh wished he brought a flashlight with him.
2) From far below, Elaine could hear whispering voices.
3) The car keys were down there somewhere.
4) The inside of the spaceship was nothing like Jennifer had expected.
5) "Help!"

Background Questions

1) Where do rhinos usually live?
2) Where are these rhinos?
3) How big is the area they have to live in?
4) Is the temperature hot or cold where they are?
5) What would their skin feel like if you could touch it?
6) Are these rhinos young, middle-aged, or old (for rhinos)?
7) If they could talk, what would their voices sound like?
8) What do they like to eat?
9) Give these rhinos names that you think say something about their personalities.
10) What do these rhinos smell like?

What's the Story?

1) Imagine this is a zoo where the rhinos aren't treated well. Write a dialogue of their conversation as they plan to escape.
2) Write an internal monologue of one of the rhino's thoughts as he or she observes the behavior of the humans watching from above.
3) Imagine this is the rhinos' first day in the zoo. Write an internal monologue of what they might be thinking.
4) Imagine this was your first day on the job and you had to bathe these rhinos. Write about what that experience would be like.
5) Write about a particularly interesting experience you had while watching animals in the zoo or in the wild.

<u>Bonus</u>: Make up your own story, poem, or essay inspired by this photo.

First Lines

1) Brady hated visiting the zoo.
2) Everyone agreed that the "buddy-system" was the best strategy.
3) The summer of 2010 was the hottest one anybody could remember.
4) "The strangest thing happened to me today," Randy Rhino said to Ruthie Rhino.
5) "Does my butt look big to you?"

Background Questions

1) How deep is the snow?
2) Where is this walkway?
3) Who shoveled the snow from the walkway?
4) How long did it take to shovel all of the snow from the walkway?
5) How cold was it on the day this photo was taken?
6) Is the walkway slippery?
7) What is the building on the far end of the walkway?
8) What time of day is it in the photo?
9) How long does it take to get from one end of the walkway to the other?
10) How often do people walk on this walkway?

What's the Story?

1) Imagine that your job is to shovel snow from the walkway. Write about what that job would be like. What would you see when you stopped to rest and looked around? Are people waiting for you to finish so they can walk here? Do you have other walkways to shovel after this one? Do you like your job?

2) Imagine someone is in the building at the far end looking out the window at someone else shoveling snow from this walkway. Write an internal monologue of the thoughts of the person as he or she watches the walkway being shoveled.

3) Write about what it would be like to slip and fall on this walkway on the coldest day of winter.

4) Imagine school was canceled because of the snow, but you didn't know it, so you and your best friend showed up anyway. Write about what you would do.

5) Write about a particularly interesting experience you had in the snow or on a very cold day.

Bonus: Make up your own story, poem, or essay inspired by this photo.

First Lines

1) In the distance, Bruce could hear the bell telling him that he was late for class again.

2) The weather report for that day was wrong.

3) This was not a good day to forget to wear shoes, but that's exactly what happened to Erica.

4) *Just a few more days,* Helen thought, *and then I can leave this place forever.*

5) "Run!"

Background Questions

1) What kind of place is beyond this sign?
2) Why are people being warned to stay away from this area?
3) Who might be working in this area?
4) What kind of work would people do in this area?
5) Who nailed the sign to the tree?
6) Who is looking in at the area from this side of the sign?
7) Why is there no fence if people are supposed to stay out?
8) Are there other signs in the area or is this the only one?
9) What kind of punishments would there be for people who cross over into this area?
10) What's the difference between, "posted," "no trespassing," and "keep out"?

What's the Story?

1) Notice that the sign sends its message in three different ways: "posted," "no trespassing," and "keep out." Imagine the sign's designer, and write a dialogue of the conversation between that designer and his or her supervisor about why the sign needs to send its message three different ways.

2) Imagine you are looking at this sign and you really want to go into the forbidden area. Write an internal monologue of your thoughts as you decide whether or not you will cross the "no trespassing" line.

3) Write about the people who work in this area. Describe them. Describe the job they're doing. Is it dangerous? Do they like their work? What do they talk about while they work? How do they feel about people not being allowed in the area where they work?

4) Write about what it would be like for two people to sneak into this forbidden area.

5) Write about an interesting experience when you went someplace you weren't supposed to go.

Bonus: Make up your own story, poem, or essay inspired by this photo.

First Lines

1) He didn't think anyone would find out.
2) Daryl was thrilled that this would be his last day at this horrible job.
3) Annette had never heard a sound like that before.
4) *Just a few more steps,* Jerry thought, *and I'll be safe.*
5) "What do you think you're doing?!"

Background Questions

1) How long has this donut shop been closed?
2) Was this a popular place to get donuts when it was open?
3) Is this donut shop in the city, a small town, or a rural area?
4) This looks like a house–does anyone live there?
5) What time of day is this?
6) Who is driving the car?
7) Where is the person in the car going in such a hurry?
8) Describe the people who used to work at the donut shop.
9) What happened to the people who worked here when the donut shop closed?
10) Why did the donut shop close?

What's the Story?

1) Write about what things were like on the last day that this donut shop was open.
2) Imagine this was you favorite place to get breakfast every morning on your way to work or school. Write about what it was like the day you discovered it had closed.
3) Imagine two people who worked in this donut shop together many years ago. Write about what they would talk about with each other if they met again now outside the closed down donut shop.
4) Describe the inside of this donut shop as it looks now with the business closed down.
5) Write about a particularly interesting experience you had while in a donut shop or fast food restaurant, either as a worker or as a customer.

<u>Bonus</u>: Make up your own story, poem, or essay inspired by this photo.

First Lines

1) Nothing lasts forever.
2) The face in the car looks strangely familiar.
3) The collapsing roof was the first sign that something was wring.
4) Starting that day, he vowed to eat a healthier diet.
5) "What was that?!"

Background Questions

1) Where is this shack?
2) How cold is it?
3) What's inside the shack?
4) Who built this shack?
5) What purpose does the shack serve?
6) Are there other building around or is the shack by itself?
7) How old is the shack?
8) How long has it been since anyone has been inside this shack?
9) Why is the door of the shack open?
10) Is the shack solid or could a person knock it down with a rock from the rock pile next to it?

What's the Story?

1) Write about someone who is lost in the woods on a frigid day and finds this shack just as he or she is about to give up hope. Focus on the thoughts and emotions that person would experience.
2) Write a dialogue between two people outside this shack. One person is afraid to go inside, but the other person is very curious and wants to check it out.
3) Imagine you are the only person in the world and you live in this shack. What would your life be like?
4) Describe what it would be like to be inside this shack during a fierce blizzard.
5) Have you ever had a place where you could go to hide out from everyone in your life? Write about why you chose that place and how it made you feel to be there. If you've never had a "hideout" of your own, write about what kind of place you would like to have had.

<u>Bonus</u>: Make up your own story, poem, or essay inspired by this photo.

First Lines

1) "Hello? Is anyone in there?"
2) The hut was a welcome sight after hiking for so long.
3) Even though years had gone by, the shack looked exactly as he remembered it.
4) There was only one place he could be hiding.
5) Joan thought the snow would never stop falling.

Background Questions

1) What does "butts" mean in this context?
2) What are some other names for cigarettes?
3) What kind of building is this ash container attached to?
4) Can you imagine what it looks like inside this ash container?
5) How often is this ash container emptied and cleaned?
6) How many people put cigarettes into this ash container every day?
7) Can you imagine what this ash container smells like?
8) What do people say about this ash container when they pass by it?
9) Does the word "butts" make you laugh?
10) What happens if it rains on this ash container?

What's the Story?

1) Imagine you are the person whose job is to clean out this ash container. Write about what that job would be like.
2) Imagine two people have just started dating, and one of them begins to smoke next to this ash container. The other one didn't know that the person they just started dating smoked. Write an internal monologue of the thoughts of the one who isn't smoking.
3) Describe someone standing alone and smoking next to this ash container. Focus on their movements, appearance, facial expressions, and mannerisms.
4) Describe the area around this ash container. What sort of building is the container attached to? What businesses are nearby? What is the traffic in the streets like? What kinds of people walk by?
5) Do you know someone who smokes? Write about what it's like to be around that person while he or she is smoking.

Bonus: Make up your own story, poem, or essay inspired by this photo.

First Lines

1) He promised this would be his last cigarette ever.
2) As Karen approached, she saw a man smoking a cigarette.
3) A crowbar should do the job.
4) "Where did you hide the diamonds?"
5) *I can't do this any more,* Bernice thought.

Background Questions

1) What kind of a building are these machines in?
2) What specific place in that building are these machines in?
3) Do these machines still work?
4) What year were these machines built?
5) How long have these machines been in this place?
6) Who put these machines here?
7) Are there any other machines stored nearby?
8) If these machines could see, what would they see from where they are?
9) Are there any sounds in the area around these machines?
10) Give these machines names?

What's the Story?

1) Imagine that the fan is visiting the typewriters after being in a modern office. Write the dialogue of a conversation where the fan tries to explain computers to the two typewriters.
2) Imagine the two typewriters are the adoptive parents of the fan. Write the dialogue of a conversation in which the typewriters tell the fan that it's adopted.
3) Imagine that these three machines are imprisoned here. Write the dialogue of their conversation as they plot their escape.
4) Imagine that a famous writer of classic books recently used the typewriter in the foreground. Write the dialogue of a conversation where they all discuss the famous writer.
5) Have you ever used an old-style typewriter? If so, describe what that was like. If not, write about what you imagine that would be like.

Bonus: Make up your own story, poem, or essay inspired by this photo.

First Lines

1) Click-clack-clickity-clack-clackity-clack-click-ding!
2) "Hey, who broke these old computers?"
3) Sometimes a priceless antique and a piece of junk are not as different as they might seem.
4) "Who's up there?!" the voice called out from below.
5) This was the strangest crime scene Detective Broxton had seen in many years.

Background Questions

1) What season of the year is this?
2) Is this a school day or a weekend?
3) How old are these busses?
4) How many busses in addition to these five are parked in this lot?
5) Where are the bus drivers?
6) Where are the kids who usually ride these busses to school?
7) When was the last time these busses did their routes?
8) When is the next time these busses will do their routes?
9) How many miles a day do these busses cover?
10) When was the last time these busses had a check up with a mechanic?

What's the Story?

1) Imagine theses busses could talk. Write a dialogue of the conversation they might have after a long day of driving their routes.
2) Describe the scene and action early in the morning as these busses all pull out from the lot to begin driving their routes.
3) Write about a group of kids who have come to this bus lot on a weekend. What would they say, do, and think without any adults around?
4) Write about a group of students who are riding in a school bus while out for a field trip. Imagine that the bus driver is lost in an area where none of them has ever been before.
5) Write about a typical, boring ride on a school bus. Try to make what you write show how boring the ride was—but write about it in a way that makes it interesting for your readers.

Bonus: Make up your own story, poem, or essay inspired by this photo.

First Lines

1) Tomorrow would be the first day of school in Barton County.
2) *No one will ever find me here,* Christopher thought.
3) "Where did you say you left the keys?"
4) "Well, I guess we'd better get started. These busses aren't going to clean themselves!"
5) When Jeff said he would be waiting in the yellow bus, Barb did realize just how unhelpful that information would be.

Background Questions

1) What ocean is in the distance?
2) Where is this beach?
3) What season of the year is this?
4) What time of day is this?
5) What is the temperature at the beach?
6) Is this day mostly sunny with a few clouds or is it just before a rainstorm?
7) Why are no people walking on the beach?
8) Are any people staying in the house in the distance?
9) What does the air smell like at this beach?
10) What sounds can be heard from this balcony?

What's the Story?

1) Imagine two people are sitting on this balcony looking out at the ocean on the last day of their vacation. Write a dialogue of their conversation.
2) Imagine two people walk out onto the balcony of the house in the distance. You can't hear or see them clearly, but they are doing something interesting. Write about your observations of them.
3) Imagine you can hear music coming from the house in the distance. What does the music tell you about the people in the house?
4) Describe a group of people participating in a fun activity on the beach.
5) Have you ever been to the beach? If so, write about an event that happened to you while visiting the beach. If not, write about what you would like to if you went to the beach.

Bonus: Make up your own story, poem, or essay inspired by this photo.

First Lines

1) After three days of rain, the morning dawned clear and warm.
2) The house looked empty.
3) *Where am I?* he thought as he awoke.
4) "Why not today?" Carol asked Ron as they sat on the balcony listening to the ocean.
5) "How did you get sand *there?*" she asked.

Background Questions

1) Give these two guys names.
2) How old are these guys?
3) What kind of building are they hanging around in front of?
4) What kind of area is this (city, town, rural, etc.)?
5) If these guys are on break from a job, what kind of job?
6) How long have they been sitting here?
7) Are these guys friends or did they just meet?
8) How would you describe their emotions?
9) Are they quiet or are they talking with each other?
10) What would you say to these guys as you drove by?

What's the Story?

1) Imagine that these guys have been working very hard at an outdoor job on a hot summer day. Write a dialogue of their conversation as they take a ten-minute break in the middle of their workday.
2) Imagine that these guys are strangers who just met here a few minutes ago. Write about how they came to be sitting together here.
3) Imagine that these guys are best friends, but they recently had an argument and aren't speaking to each other. Write an alternating monologue of their thoughts as they sit together.
4) Imagine that these guys are alien researchers from another planet sent here to blend in and observe earthlings. Write about what they might be thinking or talking about as they watch us.
5) Have you ever been in a situation where you had to spend time with a stranger? If so, write about what that situation was like. If not, write about how you think you would behave in such a situation.

<u>Bonus</u>: Make up your own story, poem, or essay inspired by this photo.

First Lines

1) This would take a lot of explaining.
2) Even his own twin brother wouldn't have recognized him.
3) Clouds gathered.
4) Joe and Ron wrestled with the age-old question: *Harry Potter* or *Lord of the Rings*?
5) The scent of fresh-cut grass hung in the air.

Background Questions

1) Give this boy a name
2) Does he seem comfortable in this chair?
3) Where is this chair?
4) Where are the boy's parents?
5) How long has he been sitting in this chair?
6) How would you describe the boy's emotions?
7) Is the boy waiting for something?
8) How old is this boy?
9) How tall is this boy?
10) How much does this boy weigh?

What's the Story?

1) Write about a young boy who has been put in a "time-out chair" because he was misbehaving.
2) Imagine this child listening to his parents having an emotional discussion. Write the dialogue of the adult conversation along with an internal monologue of the boy's thoughts as he listens and observes.
3) Write an internal monologue of an adult's thoughts as he or she watches this boy fidgeting in the chair.
4) Describe a small child climbing into an adult-sized piece of furniture or using an adult-sized tool.
5) Do you remember a moment in your childhood when everything seemed too big for you? If so, write about that experience. If not, write about what you image that experience would be like.

Bonus: Make up your own story, poem, or essay inspired by this photo.

First Lines

1) "Mom!"
2) We saw him three times that day.
3) *I'm a big boy,* Joey thought.
4) We all knew it wasn't a good idea.
5) Sharon was on the verge of panic.

Background Questions

1) Give this man a name.
2) How old is this man?
3) What sort of body of water is he wading in?
4) How long has he been in the water?
5) What season of the year is this?
6) How cold is the water?
7) What does the bottom feel like under his feet?
8) Is he looking for something in the water?
9) What is he looking for?
10) Are people on shore looking at him?

What's the Story?

1) Imagine the man has lost an object that is very important in the water. Write an internal monologue of his thoughts as he searches for it.
2) Imagine this is the hottest day of the summer. Describe how he feels inside his heavy rubber waders and boots in the cool water.
3) Imagine that the man is doing some kind of job in the water and that his boss (the kind of boss who likes to micro-manage) is on the shore. Write a dialogue of their conversation as the boss tells him what to do.
4) Write about his man trying to catch fish with only his bare hands. Describe the action in vivid detail.
5) Write about a time you lost something and had a very difficult time trying to find it.

Bonus: Make up your own story, poem, or essay inspired by this photo.

First Lines

1) There's a time and place for everything.
2) *How can I be thirsty?* Rick wondered to himself.
3) Mr. Pope was a very dedicated science teacher.
4) This is not what I had in mind.
5) "Keep trying!"

Background Questions

1) Give these two boys names.
2) Are these two boys brothers?
3) How old are these two boys?
4) What kind of place is this?
5) What season of the year is this?
6) Where are these boys' parents?
7) Are there other people around?
8) What kind of animal is this?
9) What other cut-out animals might be nearby?
10) Who is taking the boy's photograph?

What's the Story?

1) Imagine these boys are on a summer vacation trip with their families. Write about what they will tell their classmates about the trip when they go back to school in the fall.
2) Write the dialogue of these boys' conversation as they wait for an adult to get a unfamiliar or malfunctioning camera working to take their photograph.
3) Imagine that an adult without children of his or her own is watching these happy boys posing for a photograph take by their happy parents. Write an internal monologue of the thoughts the observer would have.
4) Imagine that the kangaroo cutout could actually talk. Write a dialogue of the conversation it might have with the boys when their parents aren't looking.
5) Write about a time you have been asked to pose for a photograph.

Bonus: Make up your own story, poem, or essay inspired by this photo.

First Lines

1) Aaron wondered how long the drive home would take.
2) "Hey, what kind of snake is that?"
3) They were the kind of kids who would do just about anything for a laugh.
4) *I wish birthdays happened more than once a year,* Scott thought.
5) "Please sit still!"

Background Questions

1) Give these women names.
2) How old are these women?
3) How are these women related to each other?
4) Do these women exercise regularly?
5) Why is the woman on the left using hiking poles?
6) Where are these women walking?
7) What time of day is this?
8) What season of the year is this?
9) Are there many people walking nearby, or are these women alone?
10) How far do you think they have walked?

What's the Story?

1) Imagine these two women are mother and daughter but only see each other once a year. Write a dialogue of their conversation as they walk together.
2) These women seem to be walking on a beach. Describe the beach where they are walking is great detail, including the sounds, sights, other people, and conditions. Really make your description vivid so that your readers can experience what the scene is like.
3) Write about these women being in a training program as the oldest participants ever in a 100-mile race.
4) Imagine that these women are long-time friends, but they have just had an argument and are walking in silence, angry with one another. Write an internal monologue of one or both of their thoughts as the go over the argument in their minds.
5) Think of a time when you walked a long distance and write about why you walked so far.

Bonus: Make up your own story, poem, or essay inspired by this photo.

First Lines

1) They were almost there.
2) *Those crazy kids!* Betty thought.
3) The sun beat down on them, but they kept going.
4) This was the happiest day of her life.
5) Life is full of surprises.

Background Questions

1) How big is this television?
2) How hard was it for the man to carry the television out of the roadside ditch?
3) How long had the television been in the ditch?
4) Why is this man helping to clean trash out of the ditch?
5) Is this man working by himself, or is he part of a cleanup group?
6) Give this man a name.
7) Give the person who dumped the television here a name.
8) Have other people dumped their trash here?
9) Why do people litter?
10) Why would someone dump a television here instead of disposing of it properly?

What's the Story?

1) Imagine that the television has thoughts and feelings. From the point of view of the television itself, write about being thrown away along the road?

2) Make a list of all the things you think might have been thrown away along this stretch of road. Describe each item in detail so that your readers have a vivid picture of what it looks like.

3) Put yourself in the place of the man doing the roadside cleanup. Write about what it would be like for him to haul this heavy, dirty, smelly television up out of the ditch and onto the road.

4) Put yourself in the place of the person throwing away the television. Describe what it was like to come to this place and discard it along the road.

5) Have you ever been part of a cleanup project? Write about what the experience was like for you.

Bonus: Make up your own story, poem, or essay inspired by this photo.

First Lines

1) "I'm gonna get this big baby home, plug it in, and fire it up!"

2) For the fifth year in a row year, Albert made another amazing discovery.

3) What's that sound?"

4) They finally got the time machine to work.

5) Gary started to realize what a terrible mistake he had made.

Background Questions

1) How wide is this boardwalk?
2) How far above the ground is this boardwalk?
3) Does this boardwalk feel solid or like it might collapse as you walk on it?
4) What are the weather and temperature like?
5) What can you see in the brush on either side of this boardwalk?
6) Are there other people walking somewhere on this boardwalk?
7) How far can someone walk on this boardwalk?
8) What can you hear when you are walking on this boardwalk?
9) Are there any animals around?
10) What is ahead and around the bend on this boardwalk?

What's the Story?

1) Imagine a frightening animal (maybe a bear or an alligator) is running toward you on this boardwalk. Write a narrative about what that experience would be like.
2) Write a dialogue of the conversation you might have walking on this boardwalk with someone important in your life—a parent or best friend, for example.
3) Imagine you were walking alone on this boardwalk and you fell off the side into the deep brush and mud and maybe even shallow water and you had a hard time getting out. Write a narrative of what that would be like.
4) Imagine this boardwalk is near your home and you walk on it often— but one day, something big has changed (a fallen tree across the boardwalk or a section of the boardwalk damaged by fire, for example). Write an internal monologue of your thoughts when you discover the change.
5) Have you ever walked by yourself anywhere that seems isolated and enclosed like this boardwalk? If so, write about what that was like. If not, write about what you think the experience would be like.

Bonus: Make up your own story, poem, or essay inspired by this photo.

First Lines

1) It would be dark soon.
2) Sometimes we have to make important decisions even if we don't want to.
3) He heard the footsteps before anything else.
4) Morning was her favorite time of day.
5) This was a bad time for Tom to realize he had left his cell phone in the car.

Background Questions

1) What kind or room is this?
2) Is this room part of a larger building?
3) If there are other rooms nearby, what are they like?
4) What is the building itself like?
5) What kinds of books are on the shelves?
6) Do these books stay on the shelves most of the time or do people read them frequently?
7) Make up some titles for these books.
8) Do lots of people come to this room, or is this a private space for one person?
9) What can you hear when you are in this room?
10) What can you see out the window when you sit in the chair?

What's the Story?

1) Imagine this is a bookstore or library. Write a dialogue of the conversation between two people as they look at the books. The people could be best friends, strangers, or even people who don't like each other. Have them talk about anything except the books.
2) Imagine that, when no one is around, these books secretly come alive, talk, and move around the room. Write about what they would do.
3) Imagine that you are the author of one or more of these books. Write about what it would be like to overhear people talking about one of your books.
4) Write about someone sitting at the desk, looking out the window, and trying to write something.
5) Do you have a special place where you read, study, or write? Describe what that place is like, or describe a place you would like to create for yourself.

<u>Bonus</u>: Make up your own story, poem, or essay inspired by this photo.

First Lines

1) The love letter fell from between the pages.
2) Josh had no idea how to solve the secret code.
3) She awoke as light filled the window.
4) He wondered if she would recognize him after all these years.
5) *Where could he be hiding?* Rhonda wondered.

Background Questions

1) What kind of person put up this sign?
2) What are they saying "no" to?
3) How long has this sign been in this yard?
4) What do the neighbors think of this sign?
5) How long did it take someone to make this home-made sign?
6) Does this sign make you feel different emotions compared to a sign that might say "yes"?
7) How many people see this sign every day?
8) What sort of issue do you think the sign refers to?
9) Would it be hard to change the mind of the sign owner?
10) If you were on the "yes" side of the issue, would you be tempted to tear down this sign?

What's the Story?

1) Write about going up to the front door of the house with this sign in the yard, knocking, and having a conversation with the person who answers about the sign.
2) Write an internal monologue of the thoughts of a person who puts a political sign in his or her yard.
3) Write about what you don't like, what you say "no" to. Either focus on one big thing or make a list of as many separate things as you can think of.
4) Write a dialogue of the conversation between two people stopped at a traffic light as they discuss this sign.
5) Write about a time when you had an argument with someone about a political or social issue.

Bonus: Make up your own story, poem, or essay inspired by this photo.

First Lines

1) An hour passed before he worked up the courage to step out of the car.
2) The new neighbors had seemed so nice on the phone.
3) The weather forecast called for snow.
4) She was in for a big surprise.
5) He had his answer at long last.

Background Questions

1) How many people can you see?
2) Are these people on a boat or on land?
3) What is the range of ages of these people?
4) Why do they all have binoculars?
5) Describe the weather conditions.
6) Is one of these people the leader of the group?
7) Do these people know each other or are they strangers?
8) What kind of body of water are they near?
9) What are they all looking at?
10) Are there other people outside the frame of the photograph looking at the same thing?

What's the Story?

1) Write the dialogue of a conversation between two people in this group.
2) Write the monologue of one person's thoughts as he or she eavesdrops on the other people's conversations.
3) Imagine you are in charge of this group and their sight-seeing activity, but none of them listen to you or do what you say. Write about what you would say and do in that situation.
4) Imagine that these people are here to see something like a rare bird or animal, but something totally unexpected happens, such as a UFO landing or a boat running aground. Write about what the people would see and how they would react.
5) Write about a time you waited with other people to see something special.

Bonus: Make up your own story, poem, or essay inspired by this photo.

First Lines

1) "But Mom, you said this would be fun!"
2) The note said 6 p.m.
3) Mr. Johnson was not the kind of person to make things up.
4) Wanda had never lied to her sister before.
5) "Is this your first time?"

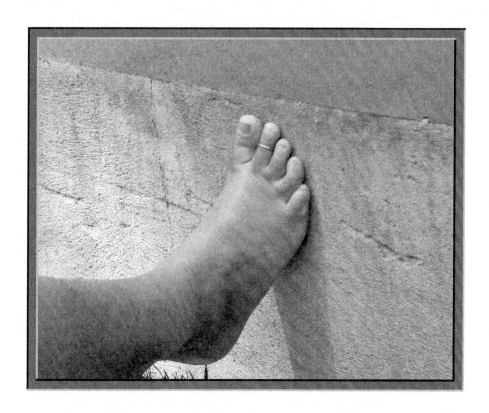

Background Questions

1) Is this a male or female foot?
2) Is this a child's or an adult's foot?
3) In what kind of place is this person displaying his or her bare foot?
4) Is the person sitting or standing on the other foot?
5) Is this foot propped against a wall or is the picture sideways and the foot on the ground?
6) What kind of ring is on the second toe?
7) How many other people are around this barefoot person?
8) What kind of shoe did the person remove to become barefoot?
9) Give names to each of the person's five toes.
10) What is the person's other foot doing?

What's the Story?

1) Write about someone who sitting in a crowded room looking at someone else's feet. Why is he or she looking at them? What is he or she thinking? How does looking at the other person's feet make him or her feel?

2) Imagine that the ring on the second toe was a gift. Write about that gift being presented.

3) Write about someone who is barefoot in an inappropriate place and/or situation.

4) Take off your shoes right now and look at your feet. If they could talk what would they say? Write the dialogue of a conversation between your left and right foot or between your feet and your brain or between your feet and someone else's feet.

5) Write about something uncomfortable that happened to your own feet: for example, stepping on something sharp, twisting your ankle, dropping something on your foot, or stubbing your toe.

Bonus: Make up your own story, poem, or essay inspired by this photo.

First Lines

1) She still had a two-hour walk ahead of her.
2) "What are you trying to tell me, Jeff?"
3) The phone call came when he least expected it.
4) Christmas was still six months away.
5) Last night he dreamed of shoes.

Background Questions

1) Is this woman giving a speech?
2) Where is she giving a speech?
3) Who is in her audience?
4) What's the purpose of her speech?
5) Has she given this speech before or is this the first time?
6) Did she choose to give this speech or is she required to do it?
7) Is she enjoying the speech or does she dislike giving it?
8) What is her name?
9) Is that an eyeball in her hand?
10) Did she make the eyeball herself?

What's the Story?

1) Imagine that this woman is in a class giving the last speech she has to give to finish her education. Write an internal monologue of her thoughts and feelings as she finishes the speech.
2) Imagine that she is giving a speech to a group of kids who don't care about the subject and are not listening to her. Describe the scene, focusing on the actions of the kids who aren't paying attention.
3) Write a script for the speech she is giving. Instead of making the speech about what seems to be obvious (that she is demonstrating how to put in a contact lens), pretend that the speech is about a subject completely unrelated to the eyeball.
4) Pretend that you are a member of the audience, but you are very distracted by something that happened to you just before you arrived for her speech. Write a monologue of your thoughts and feelings as you watch her and think about the distracting events.
5) Have you ever had to give a speech? If so, write about a particularly interesting moment from your experience giving a speech. If not, write about what you would do if you had to give a speech.

Bonus: Make up your own story, poem, or essay inspired by this photo.

First Lines

1) *I'm next*, he thought.
2) "This would be a perfect time for a fire drill," Kevin whispered.
3) The afternoon began in the usual way.
4) Sandra had considered changing careers many times before that day.
5) Sometimes five minutes can seem like five hours.

Background Questions

1) Where is this basketball hoop?
2) What month of the year is it?
3) What day of the week is it?
4) What time of day is it?
5) What is the temperature?
6) How long ago was the storm that dumped the snow here?
7) How long has it been since anyone played basketball here?
8) What activities do the kids who play basketball here in the summer do in the winter?
9) Is this hoop in a city park, a small town, or in a rural area?
10) Who lives in the house just outside the park?

What's the Story?

1) Imagine a group of kids who want to play basketball at this hoop. Write a narrative of how they would go about clearing the snow and getting ready to play.
2) Imagine that some teenagers are jumping off the piles of snow trying to dunk a basketball. Write a dialogue of their conversation as they make and miss their dunks.
3) Imagine that a person is visiting this hoop alone and thinking about a great basketball game he or she played here last summer. Write a monologue of his or her thoughts while remembering the game.
4) Picture the snowstorm that covered the area around this hoop and describe it in specific, vivid detail.
5) Recall a time you played a sport in bad weather conditions and write about that experience.

<u>Bonus</u>: Make up your own story, poem, or essay inspired by this photo.

First Lines

1) Years had passed.
2) The doctor's words still echoed in her ears.
3) "Maybe you should try again," she said.
4) One day his parents would understand.
5) "Why here?" he asked.

Background Questions

1) Give this dog a name.
2) What kind of book is the dog sitting behind?
3) Where is the person who was reading the book?
4) How long has the dog been sitting there?
5) Are there any people in the room?
6) Are there any other pets in the room?
7) What kind of room is this?
8) What kind of dog is this?
9) Is this dog happy or sad?
10) What will the dog do in the next ten seconds?

What's the Story?

1) Imagine two people walking into this room and seeing the dog looking like it is reading the book. Write a dialogue of their conversation.
2) Write about what the family cat would say if it saw this dog reading a book.
3) Write about what this dog would say if it was suddenly able to talk.
4) Pretend that the dog is reading a book about dogs. Write a monologue of the dog's thoughts as it reads the information.
5) Write about a time you saw an animal doing something that human beings usually do.

<u>Bonus</u>: Make up your own story, poem, or essay inspired by this photo.

First Lines

1) *There aren't enough pictures in this book,* Daisy thought.
2) Danielle had only been gone for five minutes.
3) "Oh my goodness!" Gary exclaimed. 'Where's my camera?"
4) No one suspected.
5) Summer vacation was almost over.

Background Questions

1) Give this guy a name.
2) Where is this?
3) What time of day is it?
4) What season of the year is it?
5) What's the weather like?
6) Has he ever made this leap before?
7) Why isn't he wearing a shirt?
8) Who is with him?
9) How far down is his landing spot?
10) What song is he listening to with his earbuds?

What's the Story?

1) Assume that he is doing this on a dare. Write the dialogue between him and his friends that led up to his leap.
2) Write his interior monologue as he prepares for his leap.
3) Describe in vivid concrete detail the physical sensations that this guy feels as he makes his leap.
4) Imagine his girlfriend and his mother are nearby. Write an alternating interior monologue as they watch him leap.
5) Have you ever done something dangerous even though you were pretty sure it was a bad idea? Write about the situation, your thoughts and feelings at the time, and what you think about it now as you reflect on what happened.

Bonus: Make up your own story, poem, or essay inspired by this photo.

First Lines

1) I wonder if she's looking at me.
2) Who would have thought such a small breeze would become so important?
3) "No one calls me chicken," Bob snarled.
4) The packed sandwiches and leftover apple pie.
5) Gravity pulls falling bodies at 13 feet per second.

Background Questions

1) Who is riding this bike?
2) What season is this?
3) What time of day is this?
4) How new is the bike?
5) Where is the rider's left hand?
6) How fast is the bike going?
7) Is the bike going uphill, downhill, or on the level?
8) Is the rider alone or with a group of people?
9) How far has the rider gone by this point in the ride?
10) Is this a recreational ride or is the rider trying to get somewhere for practical reasons?

What's the Story?

1) Imagine the rider is someone whose care has unexpectedly broken down, and he or she doesn't have the money to get it fixed. Write about the person riding to an important meeting at work rather than driving.
2) Imagine the rider is out of shape and taking up bike riding as an exercise program. Write about the first ride on the hottest day of summer.
3) Vividly describe the physical sensations of riding a bike in specific, concrete detail.
4) Write a dialogue between two bike riders, one an experienced rider who is in great shape, the other an inexperienced rider trying to keep up.
5) Many people rode bikes as part of their childhood. Write about the difference between riding a bike as a kid and riding as an adult.

<u>Bonus</u>: Make up your own story, poem, or essay inspired by this photo.

First Lines

1) The train whistle seemed far away at first.
2) Her personal ad hadn't mentioned that she liked biking.
3) The dog looked friendly.
4) "Where are your parents?"
5) This was Fred's first time inside an ambulance.

Background Questions

1) Where is this beach?
2) What are these two men's names?
3) How old are these men?
4) Do these men know each other or did they just meet on the beach?
5) What time of day is this?
6) How long have they been fishing on this day?
7) How often do they come to this beach to fish?
8) Do they live near here or are they tourists?
9) Do these men know what they're doing, or are they just pretending to be good at fishing?
10) Are the fish biting on this day?

What's the Story?

1) Write a dialogue between these two men in which they talk about anything other than fishing.
2) Imagine that these two men come here often, but on this day they see something in the ocean that they've never seen before. Write a narrative of what they do in response to the new event.
3) Imagine that one of these two men loves fishing, but the other hates it. Write an alternating monologue that shows the difference in their attitudes on this particular day.
4) Imagine that one of these men fishes here regularly and thinks of this as his spot, but on this day the other man has invaded his space. Write about that situation for the perspective of the man who thinks his space is being violated, and then from the perspective of the interloper.
5) Have you ever been fishing? If so, write about a particularly interesting event that happened while you were fishing.

Bonus: Make up your own story, poem, or essay inspired by this photo.

First Lines

1) The ocean can sometimes play tricks with a man's vision.
2) "You're not like this at the office," Ron said.
3) He didn't know how to bring up the subject.
4) It was the perfect crime.
5) Joe always thought that a "message in a bottle" was just a cliché.

Background Questions

1) Give this young man a name.
2) What city is he in?
3) Is school is he graduating from?
4) How old is he?
5) How many people are in his graduating class?
6) What was his final grade point average?
7) What was his class rank?
8) How many of his siblings graduated before or after him?
9) Who came to his graduation ceremony?
10) How long ago did he get that fantastic haircut?

What's the Story?

1) Imagine this young man is going to see his academic advisor to see if his late assignments were accepted, allowing him to graduate. Write an internal monologue of his thoughts as he anticipates and then gets the news.
2) Take the view of this young man's mother as she watches him walk away to line up for his graduation ceremony. Write a descriptive piece where you focus on her facial expressions and body language.
3) Write a narrative describing the action as this young man sprints along the street and dodges obstacles while trying not to be late for his own graduation ceremony.
4) Imagine the young man in the photo is actually looking at this photo many years after he graduated. Write a dialogue between him and his own son who is about to graduate from college.
5) Recall a graduation ceremony that you attended, either your own or someone else's. Write about one particularly significant moment during the ceremony, focusing on developing the emotional implications of the moment.

<u>Bonus</u>: Make up your own story, poem, or essay inspired by this photo.

First Lines

1) He could pull it off if he somehow managed to keep his cool.
2) "Is anyone else not wearing pants under their graduation gown?" Daryl wondered.
3) The car horn shocked him back to reality.
4) If only she could see me now.
5) To his shock, the lessons from ninth-grade algebra actually did come in handy for Roger that day.

Background Questions

1) How many pieces of pottery can be seen?
2) Who made this pottery?
3) What techniques did the potter use?
4) Are these finished pieces or still in process?
5) Where is this place?
6) What else is in the room?
7) What is the weather like outside?
8) What does this room smell like?
9) What sounds can be heard in the room?
10) Who actually sees this pottery on a day-to-day basis?

What's the Story?

1) Put yourself in the place of a craftsperson at a fir with your works for sale. Describe the people walking by, focusing on the way they look at your work as they appraise it.
2) Imagine that your job is to move all of these pieces of pottery to another location, either alone or with help. Narrate that experience.
3) Imagine that some of these pieces of pottery have the special gift of being able to come alive at night when no human beings are in the room. Write a dialogue of their conversations with one another.
4) Imagine someone who is very angry smashing these pots. Narrate that event, focusing on the sounds and visual details as the pots are smashed.
5) Have you ever done an art or craft project that was meaningful to you in some way? Reflect on what made the experience meaningful.

Bonus: Make up your own story, poem, or essay inspired by this photo.

First Lines

1) Gina had only a few minutes to find the key.
2) He lit the shop lamp at 5 a.m., just as he had nearly every morning for the last thirty years.
3) Sandy's true love was singing.
4) There are places a big dog with a happy tail shouldn't go.
5) He had served three years of a four-year sentence when they assigned him to the pottery studio.

Background Questions

1) Where is this road?
2) What's around the bend?
3) How cold is it?
4) Did the snow just start or has it been falling for a while?
5) Does it snow here often or is this unusual?
6) How far is the nearest town?
7) How long ago did the last car pass by?
8) What time of day is it?
9) When was the road last plowed?
10) What's out of frame on either side of the road?

What's the Story?

1) Imagine your car has broken down on this road in these weather conditions. Vividly describe what it would be like to walk five miles to the next town.
2) Write the dialogue of a conversation between tow people walking on this road on a warm summer day as they discuss the time they walked on this road during a terrible winter storm.
3) Narrate the action of a car chase on this road during these weather conditions.
4) Imagine a very old man or woman walking a very old dog along this road in these weather conditions. Write an alternating interior monologue of both the human and canine thoughts during the experience.
5) Reflect on a specific experience you have had with extreme weather. What made this experience memorable?

Bonus: Make up your own story, poem, or essay inspired by this photo.

First Lines

1) No matter how many times he tapped the gas gauge, it refused to budge from "E."
2) *Scrape. Scrape. Scrape.*
3) He struggled with the gloves he found under the front seat for a full minute before he realized they were a small child's gloves.
4) Linda was beginning to think that she should have gotten a ride home for winter break from someone who could hold a conversation better than Melanie.
5) He hadn't thought of that Christmas so long ago in at least twenty years.

Background Questions

1) Who lives in this house?
2) Who is present in the house at this moment?
3) What season of the year is it?
4) What time of day is it?
5) What's the weather like outside?
6) Are there any pets in the house?
7) How many steps are there in this stairway?
8) What sounds can be heard in this house?
9) Is this a new house or an old one?
10) How many rooms are there in the upstairs of this house?

What's the Story?

1) Imagine that this house is haunted but the ghosts are bored because no one is home. Write a dialogue of their conversation.
2) Imagine returning many years later as an adult to the house where you grew up. Write an internal monologue as the person explores his or her former home.
3) Imagine someone has fallen down these stairs and been injured severely and needs to get to a phone upstairs to call for help. Narrate the struggle to get up the stairs.
4) Describe the sounds coming from the upstairs as a family goes about its business getting ready for another day of work and school.
5) Have you ever been alone in a house and felt afraid? Reflect on the experience and explore the sources of your fear.

Bonus: Make up your own story, poem, or essay inspired by this photo.

First Lines

1) She had to tell him sometime.
2) Winter would arrive soon.
3) Time seemed to stand still at that moment.
4) The fifth stair always squeaked—or was it the sixth?
5) "Dinner's ready!"

Background Questions

1) How many pairs of shoes do you see?
2) How many are for adults?
3) How many are for children?
4) How many are sports shoes?
5) Why were all these shoes left here?
6) Why is the white pair set off on its own?
7) Who owns these shoes?
8) How many people live in this house?
9) Where are those people right now?
10) What shoes are they wearing instead of these?

What's the Story?

1) Imagine these shoes are living beings and the wooden box in the corner is their divinity. Write a narrative of what they are doing as they assemble here.
2) Imagine the family who lives here has mysteriously disappeared and you are a detective sent to investigate their empty house. Write an internal monologue of the detective's thoughts while pondering these shoes abandoned in the entryway.
3) Narrate a story of the family pets ripping and chewing these shoes in a playful frenzy.
4) Write a dialogue of the family discussion happening around the kitchen table not far inside the door of this house.
5) If you're reading these words, there's a pretty strong chance that you worn shoes. What do your shoes say about you? Reflect on how many shoes you own, what kinds you have, why you bought them, how often you wear them, how you get rid of them, etc.

Bonus: Make up your own story, poem, or essay inspired by this photo.

First Lines

1) "Mom!"
2) Toni hadn't returned to her parent's home in more than a year.
3) Christmas came early to the Anderson household that year.
4) "If the shoe fits," he said, knowing it was a cliché but not caring.
5) The first phone call came at 5 a.m.

Background Questions

1) Where is this?
2) Give the bear a name.
3) How often does the bear cross here?
4) Who put up this sign?
5) How long has the sign been here?
6) How often do people stop and look at this sign?
7) What is the sign made of?
8) Give the sign maker a name.
9) What other animals cross here?
10) What sort of a neighborhood is this?

What's the Story?

1) Imagine that you are the person who made this sign. Write an interior monologue of your thoughts as you constructed the sign.
2) What would the bear do if it saw this sign (assuming the bear could read it)? Narrate the bear's actions during the encounter.
3) Write a dialogue between a couple as they drive by the sign. Have them argue about the likelihood of a bear crossing here, and then narrate the action as a bear cross directly in front of their car.
4) Narrate the story of the person taking the picture of the bear that became part of the sign.
5) Have you had any particularly interesting encounters with wildlife? Reflect on the experience, emphasizing the emotions and actions of the events.

Bonus: Make up your own story, poem, or essay inspired by this photo.

First Lines

1) We all have crosses to bear, or, in this case, bears to cross.
2) I love my neighborhood.
3) With the moon hidden behind thick clouds, the night was especially dark.
4) "Holy crap, did you see that?"
5) I had always been told that Bigfoot was just a myth.

Background Questions

1) Where is this?
2) What time of day is this?
3) How many mailboxes are there?
4) How deep is the snow?
4) How many stops does this mail carrier make in a day?
6) How many pieces of mail are being delivered in this stop?
7) What is the proportion of junk mail, bills, and personal correspondence in this delivery?
8) Give the mail carrier a name.
9) How long has he or she been delivering on this route?
10) What's the traffic like in this neighborhood?

What's the Story?

1) Put yourself in the place of the mail carrier. Write an internal monologue as he or she delivers the mail and speculates on what the neighborhood residents are like based on what they get in the mail.

2) Describe the interior of the mail truck in detail. What are some of the obvious things you'd expect about the interior of a mail truck? What are some surprises we might find?

3) The post office's unofficial motto is "Neither snow, nor rain, nor heat, nor gloom of night, stays these couriers from the swift completion of their appointed rounds." Narrate the story of a mail carrier who finds him or herself in weather conditions so terrible that he or she simply can't deliver the mail.

4) Write a fictional family holiday newsletter from a ridiculously dysfunctional family.

5) We've all sent or received important mail at one time or another, either actual paper mail or the electronic variety? Reflect on a time when you had an important communication through the mail, focusing on what you read into someone else's words and what you tried to communicate with your own.

Bonus: Make up your own story, poem, or essay inspired by this photo.

First Lines

1) Mrs. Johnson hadn't picked up her mail for a full week.

2) No one told Kevin about the dog.

3) Brenda heard the kids, but she didn't even sense the snowball until it hit her squarely in the face.

4) The next idiot who tells me that snow in New England disproves global warming gets a punch in the nose.

5) The day began quietly enough.

In text on the planks:

IN MEMORY OF NORMAN & JEAN RENK
PENNY & BILL — NORVA & DON
FRIENDS FOREVER
NICOLE & CLIFF CRAZY♡

BOB♡BRATSCH 1933♡2001
DAVID & ALAYNE ANDERSON ♡
ALEX, AMY, & JONATHAN NEAL 2001
PAT I WILL LOVE YOU ALWAYS~CHARLES
LOVING MEMORY OF PAT BROWN♡
ALL OF US WHO KNEW & LOVED

Background Questions

1) Where is this boardwalk?
2) How old are these planks?
3) How many people are walking here?
4) How old are the people walking here?
5) Are the people walking here strangers, friends, or family members?
6) Is this boardwalk solid or rickety?
7) How often do people visit this boardwalk?
8) How recently were these planks carved?
9) Why is one plank blank?
10) Who carves these planks?

What's the Story?

1) Imagine two people walking along this boardwalk making up stories based on the names they see in the boardwalk. Write a dialogue of their conversation as they try to make up more outlandish stories than the one before.
2) Imagine a family is walking along this boardwalk. Write about how the parents would explain to the children what the names on the planks mean.
3) Write a poem using all the names, dates, and words you can see in this photo.
4) Write a story in which two people argue about what the plank they're planning for a love one should say.
5) If you could dedicate a plank in a boardwalk like this to someone, who would it be? Write about what that person did for you to show why he or she deserves to be remembered like this.

Bonus: Make up your own story, poem, or essay inspired by this photo.

First Lines

1) "Oh, no!" she cried. "They spelled it wrong!"
2) The plank had faded since the last time she saw it.
3) The sun beat down on the back of his neck.
4) We all know how tricky memory can be.
5) Gary had carved his last plank.

Background Questions

1) What kind of room is this?
2) What's the temperature in the room?
3) What time of day is it?
4) What does the fan sound like?
5) How many speed settings does the fan have?
6) What speed is it set on in the photo?
7) Is this fan new or old?
8) How long has it been running?
9) Who is in the room?
10) Do the people in the room notice the fan?

What's the Story?

1) Imagine this fan is above a private detective's desk. Describe the office and write the dialogue between the detective and client.
2) Two lovers lie on a motel room bed in the middle of a weekday afternoon. One sleeps and the other is wide awake, staring at this ceiling fan. Write the internal monologue of that person's thoughts.
3) Imagine you are a student waiting to speak with a professor in whose class you are on the brink of certain failure. The semester is almost over, and it's the last class you need to graduate. Imagine you're sitting beneath this fan outside the professor's office door. Reflect on why you failed the class and what you need to do to make things right.
4) Start with someone bursting into an empty motel room. Narrate what happens next.
5) Have you ever stayed in a cheap, sleazy motel room alone and far from home? Reflect on what brought you to those circumstances.

Bonus: Make up your own story, poem, or essay inspired by this photo.

First Lines

1) Ben shivered, but sweat beaded on Joe's forehead.
2) No matter how often she counted the money, she always came up more than $5,000 short.
3) The trip seemed like such an adventure in the brochure.
4) One thought kept bouncing around his brain: *Who installs a ceiling fan without an on/off switch?*
5) The whirring of the ceiling fan made the silence after her question seem so much more depressing.

About the Author

John Sheirer has been teaching college writing for three decades, including more than twenty years as a full-time faculty member at Asnuntuck Community College in Enfield, Connecticut, where he has served as Writing Coordinator and Liberal Arts Department Chair. He has been honored multiple times with inclusion in *Who's Who Among America's Teachers*, and won the Distinguished Service and Educational Excellence Award at Asnuntuck.

His books include the memoirs, *Growing Up Mostly Normal in the Middle of Nowhere* and *Loop Year: 365 Days on the Trail*, a short story collection, *One Bite: Stories for Short Attention Spans, Stolen Moments, and Busy Lives*, a collection of essays on current events, *Tales of a Real American Liberal*, and a collection of photos and life lessons coauthored with his dog, *Libby Speaks: The Wit and Wisdom of the World's Wisest Dog*. He's a winner of the Connecticut Green Circle Award, and his books have been honored as a finalist for the Sante Fe Writers Project Literary Award, the Next Generation Indie Book Award, the International Book Award, and the Eric Hoffer Book Award. John's essays, short stories, poems, and photographs have appeared in hundreds of print and online publications, and he is a regular columnist on politics and current events for his hometown newspaper, the *Daily Hampshire Gazette*.

He is a frequent guest on political podcasts, and the Facebook page for his book *Tales of a Real American Liberal* has more than 10,000 followers and recently won the Blue Book Good Pagekeeping Award.

John lives in Northampton, Mass. with his wonderful wife Betsy and literary Border Terrier Libby. He has two fantastic grown-up stepchildren and recently became a first-time grandfather. You can find him at JohnSheirer.com, and you can find more of his photographic writing prompts at the Facebook page, *What's the Story?*

A Message from John Sheirer

Dear Reader,

I hope that reading this book has been a good experience for you. If it has, I expect that you can think of other people who would appreciate it. Here's how you could help them and me. Many books are competing for readers' attention, and the most important way for a book to get more notice is for readers to write favorable reviews and post them on Amazon.com.

The more positive reviews or comments a book gets, the more it moves up the ranking for exposure when people search on Amazon. When a book has ten reviews it becomes eligible to be included in the "also bought" and "you might like" recommendations. These listings add to the number of books likely to be purchased and read.

If you don't want to write a review, please take a few minutes to read and rate reviews posted by other readers. Just the act of "liking" a review moves books up the queue in which they appear.

Thanks in advance for your effort to boost the distribution and exposure of this book! I really appreciate it!

CPSIA information can be obtained
at www.ICGtesting.com
Printed in the USA
LVOW13s1434190118
563211LV00013B/225/P